Low-Risk Investing

Treasury Bonds, Tax Lien Certificates, Certificates of Deposits, Money Markets & Compound Interest

John I Osborne

"Peace To The Mind is a way of life. We encourage our readers to be the ruler of their universe. Control your mind and body by mastering your thoughts and actions in a positive way". Jon Frost

Books by John I Osborne

Tax Lien Certificates: Top Investment Strategies That Work,

Tax Lien Certificates: Wealth Management,

Low Risk Investing: Treasury Bonds, Tax Lien Certificates, Certificates of Deposits, Money Markets & Compound Interest, Mortgage Notes & Tax Lien Certificates Investing: Guide To Building Wealth,

Tax Lien Certificates & Tax Deed Investing: Learn How to Build Wealth and Protect Your Finances(Spanish Translation),

Low Risk Investing Extreme: 401K, Tax Lien Certificates, Index Funds, ETFs, REITs, Mutual Funds, Stock Portfolio and Retirement

www.peacetothemind.us

jonfrost@peacetothemind.us

Table of Contents

Description	5
Introduction	6
Chapter 1: Tax Liens Certificates	8
The Tax Lien Process	8
Liquidity Elements	9
Direct Investment	9
How to Bid and How It Works	10
Researching the Tax Sale Property before the Auction	10
Phase 2: Consider the Auction Fees and Deposits	11
Phase 3: Bid at the Tax Lien	11
Getting To Know the Bidding Formats	11
• Bidding Higher than the Price	11
• Bidding on the premium actions	12
• Bidding Down on the Interest Rates	12
Buying the Tax liens after the event	12
Waiting During the Redemption Periods after the Time of the Sale	13
Phase 5: Profit with Tax Liens	13
Benefits and Disadvantages of Using Tax Liens	14
Pros	14
Cons	15
Doing Your Due Diligence	15
Chapter 2: Certificates of Deposit	16
Dealers	16
How They Are Set	16
CD Laddering	17
When to Buy a CD	17
Investing in a Certificate of Deposits while Rates are Low	17
Strategies when using CDs	18

Using Short Maturities	18
Evaluating Options like the Bumping up of the Certificate of Deposit	18
Use of Short CD Laddering	18
Consider Indexed or Structured CDs	19
Being Aware Of Early Withdrawal Penalties	19
Take Care When Stretching For Yield	19
Barbell Strategies	20
Shopping Around	20
Mistakes to Avoid With Certificates Of Deposit	20
Do Not Buy Long-Term CDs Which You Cannot Exit	20
Placing Revenue into the Wrong CDs	20
Putting All the Funds in One Place	21
Letting you CD roll over automatically	21
Benefits and Disadvantages of CDs	21
CD Interests Can Get Higher Than the Savings Account Rates	21
Fixed rate of interest	21
Building Interest with a CD ladder	22
Capitalizing On the Fixed Interest Rates When the Market Drops	22
Low-Risk Investments with FDIC Insurance	22
Disadvantages	22
Locked rates	23
Time deposit limits the ability to adjust investment strategy	23
Index-linked CDs	23
Chapter 3: Money Markets	24
What is a money market?	24
Money Market Instruments	24
Money Market Accounts	26
Advantages of Money Market Accounts	27
Disadvantages of Money Market Accounts	28
Money Market Funds	29
Advantages of Money Market Funds	29
Disadvantages of Money Market Funds	29
Chapter 4: Compound Interest	31
Things That Determine the Compound Interest Returns	32
Compound interest and the time value for revenue	32

Compound Interest over the course of time	32
Benefits and disadvantages of compound interest	33
The Concept	33
Practical considerations	33
Saving benefits	33
Dividend Investing	34
Disadvantages: When It Becomes an Issue	34
Chapter 5: Treasury Bonds	35
How the Bond Pays Interest	35
How the Interest Rates Affect the Prices of the Bond	35
Why Invest In Them	36
Bond Investment and Other Strategies	37
Preserving the Principal and Earning Interest	37
Management of the Interest Rate Risk	37
Maximization of income	38
Total Return	38
Tax-Advantaged Investment	39
Pros of Treasury Bonds	39
Cons of treasury bonds	39

© Copyright 2018 - Peace To The Mind - All rights reserved

Professionals should be consulted as needed prior to undertaking any of the action endorsed herein.

This declaration is deemed fair and valid by both the American Bar Association and the Committee of Publishers Association and is legally binding throughout the United States.

Furthermore, the transmission, duplication or reproduction of any of the following work including specific information will be considered an illegal act irrespective of if it is done electronically or in print. This extends to creating a secondary or tertiary copy of the work or a recorded copy and is only allowed with an express written consent of the Publisher. All additional rights reserved.

The information in the following pages is broadly considered to be a truthful and accurate account of facts and as such any inattention, use or misuse of the information in question by the reader will render any resulting actions solely under their purview. There are no scenarios in which the publisher or the original owner of this work can be in any fashion deemed liable for any hardship or damages that may befall them after undertaking information described herein.

Additionally, the information in the following pages is intended only for informational purposes and should thus be thought of as universal. As befitting its nature, it is presented without assurance regarding its prolonged validity or interim quality. Trademarks that are mentioned are done without written consent and can in no way be considered an endorsement from the trademark holder.

Introduction

Not many people are willing to take their money or income and put them on investments such as in the shares, bonds or on the stock market. They are hesitant, especially an ordinary individual, not only because of the little knowledge that they have about investing but also because of the widely spread information that investing in such are too risky. They would often just put their money into a savings account, which they don't realize is a type of investment as well, though with not so high gains. However, with the right knowledge and understanding, people will realize that risks can be avoided, especially when you know what to look for and how to manage your accounts and assets. Also, not all investment has high risks. There are also some kinds of investments that are typically low on risks. This type of low-risk investment will be tackled in this book and one that should be greatly considered trusting your money into. Not only will you realize that investing can definitely give you an extra income and a reassurance for your future, but you would also find it fun and enjoyable, especially when you start reaping what you sow.

Investing concerns the buying and selling of investment products such as shares and bonds which are bought and sold on the exchange. The value of the investment product is particularly dependent on several elements like demand and supply. On the other hand, if the supply outweighs the demand, the value of the investment product is going to go up. Through the means of investment, one may get a higher level of return on money than if it had been deposited into a savings account. On the other hand, investment is riskier as compared to saving. Before starting to invest, there are a few things that one has to take into account. For example, you need to ask questions about your financial position, the amount of risk that you can afford, and how much knowledge and experience you have about investing activities and the financial markets. The objective of this book is to provide the tips toward low-risk investing, and this is going to concern things like treasury bonds, tax liens certificates, the certificates of deposits, and money markets.

Each concept will be discussed with concern to the different strategies and best-applied fields for each. The rate of return and the mode of investment will also be considered, not to mention the advantages and disadvantages of each mode. Deciding to invest your money is an indication that you are willing to accept certain levels of risk. Preferences are going to determine how high or low the level of risk is going to be. One can minimize their level of risk by making sure that the investment portfolio is diversified.

Investment risks are thus inherent when it comes to investments of any sort. Making an investment in assets that are low-risk and have a low rate of return is a part of the safe choices for being risk-averse. Though, you need to consider that low-risk investment has low return expectations accordingly. The other trade-off when it comes to low-risk investing is that it needs jurisdiction that is favorable on a sound property. The investor can profit from a secured loan to the taxing identity. Then, when the owner pays the taxes required to the municipality, the interest and the repayment set by the law would be paid to the investor by the property owner, who then decides to redeem the property. At the time the tax lien is issued on sound properties, the investor can profit regardless of whether the debt has been repaid or if the lien goes into foreclosure and sale.

The convenient thing is that you do not need a real estate license. There is no need for an LLC and no need for a huge starting capital in order to invest in deeds or capital. When buying the tax lien, you have basically paid the tax debt for the proprietor in exchange for certificates. The certificate can be equated to the amount of money which has been paid along with the interest. The other thing is that the investment also happens to be backed with the collateral of the property, not to mention the state laws which mandate the redemption of the tax lien certificate along with the interest and the penalty. As the investor, one is going to pay for the tax debt and locking a provided interest rate on the investment. The tax lien is one of those negotiable instruments, though there is no secondary market apart from eBay maybe.

The certificate provides evidence to the authorities that the holder has bought an enforceable interest earning lien for the property. It is a legal obligation to the first position lien on the property. It would indicate that it is the first obligation of the debt which is paid if the property goes through the process of foreclosure.

Liquidity Elements
Government agencies have annual budgets which assume predictable tax incomes. The unpaid taxes generate what is known as a shortfall. In the same way, a government agency can partially remedy this in order to sell tax liens created by debts and recorded on these properties to the investors at the auction. The agency would then be able to recoup some of the lost tax revenue. The liens and the deeds can be sold live or they can be provided at an internet-based auction. These are basically given at face-value discounts in order to make the sales much more attractive and create revenues in a faster manner.

Direct Investment
Tax deed investing or tax liens appear to be one of the more indirect methods of investing in real estate. The right to collect on tax liens is referred to as direct investment through means of a recorded interest in the property for repayment of the amount which was owed in addition to the penalties along with the related interest. The original owner of the property, when it comes to tax default, will not be able to sell the property without having to first pay off the principal or the taxation which is owed as well as the penalties and mortgage loans outstanding and the interest set by the statute. Collecting and buying on the basis of tax lien redemption may be profitable when it comes to the short-term investment and with the right advice on strategy. The other question is if the owner does not ever try to pay off the lien. In that case, the holder of the lien would be within their rights to foreclose the property in order to collect on their investment. In the worst case scenario, the investor gets their money back with interest payments which could be anywhere between 15 to 20 percent.

Hearing that a tax lien investor would have the ability to make more than 24 percent on the redeemed liens is a dream for most people and sounds a bit too good to be true. In fact, each country and state has a set of laws and procedures that support the creation of tax liens, along with the collection of the investor returns. These may be subject to alteration frequently, though. As such, the buying and management of investments within these fields appear overwhelming to the majority of the novice investors for tax liens and tax deeds. Investment within the field needs knowledge and experience and continuing research. The magic when it comes to tax lien investing is focusing on the states and counties that have the highest interest yield tax liens and where the highest amount of equity is needed in order to secure the lien. The other thing is the high yield compounding effects by reinvesting on the redemption proceeds in more tax liens.

Do not invest in tax liens thinking that you are there to get a property at a rate that would be considered as a fire-sale rate. Ninety-eight percent of the property owners usually regain possession of the property before foreclosure starts at the time the tax foreclosure begins. A lot of the tax foreclosures usually occur on land which is vacant. As such, the foreclosure can be time-consuming and a bit expensive. The other thing is that you have to ascertain the place at which you can operate. You would want to see how the process of sales and auction works and how to easily get the returns in the event of buying the certificates within the location. For some time, many counties treated tax sales as the issue to complete, so there could be bureaucracy as you proceed in this investment process. Though, the increase in platforms online has improved the process by enabling the counties to reach more people and so more places could easily participate with their improved sales. Though investors may look at tax lien investing as a kind of short-term CD and one of the safe means, they are a bit different. Tax liens are considerably high touch. There is a bit off-monitoring concerning the tax liens. The certificates should always be checked if they are already re-attained and followed-up in case something needs to be done.

How to Bid and How It Works

Most counties hold the tax lien sale on a yearly basis. A lot of auctions are done on online platforms. In Baltimore for example, the sale happens in June and the city sale is done in mid-May. You register a few weeks ahead of the actual sale and then pay $100 for the registration fee. Then, you will get an email containing a bid identification number. When the auction opens, you can bid on the certificates that interest you through an online platform. The minimum bid necessary in order to buy a tax lien certificate would be inclusive of the penalties, gross tax, and the related interest. The penalties are inclusive of applicable posts concerning the tax lien certificate sale. The minimum bid would be listed alongside the defaulted property ID number and its address. As such, the first step entails learning how to research the properties of interest. Then one learns how to participate in the various forms.

Researching the Tax Sale Property before the Auction

When people bid on tax sale property, it does not necessarily mean that you would sidestep any research. You would want to know what you are getting into and proceed to the auction with a list that meets the bidding criteria that you have already set. You can use the 4 keywords below when doing your research:

- County treasurer - this is where the sale is done and they would have the list of properties slated for the tax sale auction even before the auction.
- County assessor - when you have parcels of interest, use the office of the county assessor to investigate their potential value.
- County recorder- here you will be able to investigate whether there are other liens, judgments or even claims such as an existing tax lien or an IRS lien that is set against the property. These issues are common when it comes to tax defaulters. One might not want to place a bid on the property with a lot of claims against it.
- County surveyor- in the event that you have found listings concerning interest, one is able to look up the plot maps and the aerial views in order to see if they ought to be considered. A lot of the tax sale parcels happen to be landlocked, and they are unusually structured as they are miles away from any development which makes them not worth a lot.

Phase 2: Consider the Auction Fees and Deposits

Fees: These are the non-refundable types of charges. Some of the jurisdictions place a fee to the bidders if only just to participate. The others can charge only against the main bids. In either case, the amount of the fees has to be accounted into the yield. Several jurisdictions within counties in Arizona, for example, charge a non-refundable fee to the amount of $125 to $150 to participate in the annual certificate sales.

Deposits: These are the fees which are refundable. It is a way for the counties to participate and to make sure they are serious about the bids. The deposits are usually refunded at the end of the auction to those who did not bid as well as those who did not win. For those who bid, the deposits are usually subtracted from the winning bid such that the buyer would only owe what remains. In states like California, the deposits imposed are from $2,500 to $5,000.

Phase 3: Bid at the Tax Lien

Once there is a list of potential properties, you can then go to the auction. You could be a participant in a live sale at the county courthouse or on another place. You can also bid online using the county's designated system.

Getting To Know the Bidding Formats

Over the years, a number of states and local jurisdictions have adopted different means that bidders can use. These include:

- **Bidding Higher than the Price**
  This would be the traditional auction format where the bidders are competing by increasing the prices against each other. In every tax sale, the opening bid tends to be set

at the amount of due taxes added to the accumulated interest and the penalties. When it comes to this kind of auction, the bidders may then increase their offering price. When it comes to the deed scenarios, the figure is a representation of the amount that the bidder would pay in the event the property is foreclosed upon. For the liens, that would be the figure that the bidder would tie within the certificate. The interest is usually still based according to the figure of the back taxes and the fees or interest that is needed, so, the more that the investor bids, the lower the yield would be.

- **Bidding on the premium actions**
  There are states which prefer the traditional auction bidding procedure and have adopted a bid premium so as to counter the loophole which enabled bidders to increase the bid with no realistic ceiling. This is to assist in stopping $200,000 bids on $100,000 properties which make zero sense as bidders know that in the bidding process, they really do not have to pay. The bid premium refers to a percentage of the figure that is bid over the market value of the property. Like for example, Maryland levies the bid premium such that if a person bids $200,000 on a house that is only worth 100,000, then they would have to give $30,000 to the county as well as any amount that would be required in interest/penalties and back taxes. This premium is held without interest wherein the owner either redeems or the property goes into foreclosure. In either case, it is better to keep the bid tied at about $30,000 without interest to keep the bids realistic.

- **Bidding Down on the Interest Rates**

  This is an accepted bidding procedure in a lot of states because this is what competitors do. They bid downwards on the interest that they would like to accept. In Arizona for example, the set interest is at 16% and so, the bidders compete so they can work this backward. It is not really unusual to see the bidders even accept interest rates that are as low as 5%.

Buying the Tax liens after the event

In many places, the tax sale is not the only time where one can purchase tax foreclosed real estate. Several tax-defaulted properties do not ever get sold at the auction. Many of the counties and the municipalities employ different methods of disposing these. This can happen in two ways:

- County held property sales: When it comes to deed states, the property which is not disposed at the auction becomes owned by the municipality or the country and is usually placed on sale. Even in the lien states, when the unsold liens reach expiry, then the properties are reverted to the governing authority.

- Over-the-counter tax lien certificate sales: In the lien state, if the governing authority ends up with tax liens that are not sold, they usually make them available through what is known as 'over-the-counter' sales. The purchaser may get a county-held certificate after the auction for the amount of back taxes, penalties, and interest accumulated. There is no bidding at this time, as it is usually first come-first served.

Waiting During the Redemption Periods after the Time of the Sale

Because in a lot of jurisdictions, the tax liens have particular procedures which allow the owners of the property to make good on their debt and reclaim their property, the next thing to do would be to just wait. At times, the period of redemption could be limited to a few months up to a few years. During this interval, the proprietor may decide to redeem. You cash out and get the bid plus any interest which had accrued up until that point as well as the penalties when you were holding the lien. You should note that in the event the owner does not redeem, you can request for a foreclosure process in order to get the title deed to the property.

Phase 5: Profit with Tax Liens

Profiting from tax liens certificates is falls into 3 groups. These include earning the penalty income, earning interest, and potentially acquiring the property for the amount of back taxes owed.

Penalties: A number of states impose a penalty in addition to interest on the owner of that property. These penalties go to the one that bought the tax lien. The penalty revenue can increase your returns to a level of 40 percent of the initial investment depending on the location of the investment and on the situation at hand.

Interest: When it comes to tax lien certificates, the objective would be to earn a healthy interest rate on the amount of purchase. The interest rates can go as high as 12 to 16 percent depending on the jurisdiction. The return comes with a limited amount of risk because the liens would be backed by the municipality, and there is no fluctuation within the market.

Acquiring the below-market property: The objective of tax deed investment, is to get a property below the assigned value of the market. Though, only about 1 percent of the tax liens only go to the foreclosure. In some jurisdictions, foreclosure is a simple enough process that concerns tax deeds or the sheriff's deed. Elsewhere, it consists of a complex procedure which needs legal staff.

Benefits and Disadvantages of Using Tax Liens

Pros

Misfits

There are properties that the owner does not want. It could be that it is undeveloped or it is far from other infrastructure. It would not only be hard to sell the land or what it produces, but it is also not accessible. These properties are referred to as misfits. They are the raw land or vacant land. They represent the things the owners themselves do not want. These are the properties where owners wouldn't want to pay thousands of dollars per year, so they decided that the city should just take it back. No one ends up paying the taxation and no one buys at the tax deed sale. These are the properties that are easily owned, developed, and overturned back to the city or a corporation as expansion takes place. It would be a long-term investment though but would definitely have a good pay off in the end.

No loan against the property

A lot of the times, these properties do not have loans on them. The number of people who get a loan or a home loan to buy the property usually mortgage the company through payment of taxes each year as well as through related insurance. Even when the homeowner does not pay the mortgage, the bank will still issue payment for the property taxes and the insurance. Usually, when there is a loan against the property, the taxes are typically being paid, and so you will not see these property tax lien issues. In the event the property is owned free and clear, then you can run into that. The question though is which properties are owned free and clear. Obviously, they are those which have been owned for a long time by the owner and they have paid the loan off. Sometimes, when the property is inherited by an heir, they will not most likely pay the taxes considering they had just inherited the property. They may not also have that extra revenue every year to pay the taxes.

You may become the owner

This would be dependent on the state. In Florida for example, if the individual does not pay their taxes for a period of three years, then it is going to go to a tax deed foreclosure auction. The only means one can get it back as the tax lien owner is if no one bids at the auction. This is a bit scary because that would mean that no one wanted it in the first place. All of a sudden, you would then become stuck with a property that you do not want and now you have to pay the taxes. As such, you could potentially get stuck with one of these. If you are interested in tax liens, then you are going to have to evaluate each of the properties individually to see the one you would like to potentially buy the tax lien for.

Cons

Accumulated taxation debt

There are particular situations where the taxation debt would accumulate on the property. This is particularly common among owners that are letting their property go into taxation default, and do not resolve the matter which results in taxation debt. For example, a not so convenient building costing $4,000 is going into tax foreclosure for a period of 6 years while accumulating $600 in back taxation for each year. That would mean there is at least $3,600 accumulated tax debt on a parcel which is valued at only $4,000. If you had not done your research, and then by mistake bid upwards by $600 on that lot, there would be zero profit from that particular situation.

Bankruptcies

These are one of the legal loopholes which can cause issues concerning tax sale for the real estate investors. A bankruptcy can stop any collection effort regardless of whether it is for the interest and penalties or if it is for foreclosing on the complete default. The great news is that tax liens are priority claims. So when the bankruptcy is being resolved, you will be one of the first to be issued payment. Of course, there is no telling how much this is going to be.

Junk Property

If you do not do the due diligence on the property you are bidding on, there is a good chance that you will end up placing your finances into a sinkhole. That equates to not being able to retrieve your funds. For example, you may invest within a tax lien for what was previously a junkyard. The owners do not redeem and so you would not earn any interest. When it comes to foreclosure, you then come to the realization that there is no probable chance of being able to resell the land even if you acquire it for the amount of back taxes that your bid represents. Because it is not desirable, it could be that you will not have the chance to ever sell the property. As a matter of fact, this could be the very reason that it ended up in the tax default position in the first place.

Doing Your Due Diligence

This is the most significant thing one can do when it comes to securing a tax lien. It would be advisable to drive by and see the property for yourself as one of the steps in doing your online research. You will probably not be able to inspect the property from the inside as the homeowners would not likely give you permission to drop by whenever you want and look things up and down. Though, you would still want to know as much as possible about the property, the environment, and its history. A number of tax liens can be bought on the same property for subsequent taxpayers as well. It all depends on the length of the duration of the redemption period. As such, in a state with a redemption period that goes up to three years, three taxation liens could be bought. These taxation liens may be purchased through the same investor or via different individuals. That is an indication that you could need more capital the process continues on.

Chapter 2: Certificates of Deposit

Certificates of deposits are insured through the FDIC deposits given by the banking institutions and brokerage firms. These are promissory notes that the issuing bank delivers. Basically, one is loaning their money to the banking institution, which in turn, is going to pay back at the end of a period. These carry fixed interests and they can be accessed with ease. A lot of the time, certificates of the result is carrying fixed interest ratings which are easy to open. The rate of the return is higher as there is a higher amount of deposit. They are relatively safe as investments and so the rate of return may not be as aggressive as the other investment accounts. Usually, a longer term means a higher rate of return.

Certificates of deposits are available for terms that are as short as days, and they can even be as long as eight years. Though, the ones taken for a period of three to twelve months and between three and five years are the most common. A number of daily newspapers both on the local and national front carry information pertaining to the certificate of deposit rates, not to mention compiling the lists of offerings from the local financial institutions and national high rate leaders. The banks are aggressive advertisers in newspapers so someone keen can find a good offer on the paper. The internet is also a very good source. As such, they are popular as saving tools for the small investor. When the rates are increasing, the investors may go to the certificates of deposits but would probably not buy stocks or bonds. This, in turn, could be one of the negative signals to these markets.

Dealers

There should be about 25 dealers that issue certificates of deposits that are active within the domestic CDS for the financial institutions included among the leading groups. The function of these dealers is to distribute CDs at retail by either taking the new issues or being brokers and supporting the secondary market by selling the certificates of deposits. The bidding prices may be maintained on a consistent basis and the usual spread would be done between 5 and 10 points, though there are narrower spreads. The market for the certificates of deposits provided domestically has developed because of the effects of interest rate regulation.

How They Are Set

The banks utilize the funds from issuing the CDs in order to hold in reserve, lend or even spend for their particular activities. However, they have a number of options available. These are the options which determine the interest ratings that the banks pay on the CDs. The Fed Fund Rate happens to be the lowest cost source for funding. The central bank of the country, the Federal Reserve, is the one that sets this rate. However, the banks are also able to utilize the fed funds in order to meet the reserve requirement for that night. For the other requirements, the banks can borrow from each other at the LIBOR rate. This stands for the London Interbank Offer Rate. The bank pays this rate in one-month, six-month, one-year or five-year loans. They can pay more for the LIBOR than they would for the CDs. However, the CDs may cost more considering they have to administer them. They can just wire the loans to each other and also borrow much more than the usual CD deposit. The rates are for the certificate of deposit would, in turn, be lower as compared to what they charge their clientele to lend revenue known as the prime rate considering the banks themselves have to make a profit. Their revenue originates from the interest that is given by the ones who borrow. The costs are the interest that is paid to the lenders like the depositors in the money markets, other banks, as well as, the deposits in the CDs. Then, the rates paid on the CDs end up being higher than the fed funds rate. However, it is also lower as compared to the prime rate.

CD Laddering

Before arriving at the decision to get a certificate of deposit, it would be better to seriously consider what laddering entails and how to use it in order to decrease your exposure. Laddering means you are able to own CDs that have different maturities but they are set according to different rungs. Each rung illustrates different certificates of deposits and has a long-term as they progress to the next. You may place $200,000 on a 3-year CD and it pays 10%. Consider how you would feel if the interest rate for the 3-year CD would go up to 12% in the next year. You would be locked at 2.5% for 3 years and not be able to withdraw without incurring a penalty. When it comes to laddering, you may alternatively decide to buy five CDs and the revenue of 200,000 dollars. You may place $50,000 in the first year of the CD, 60,000 dollars in the second year of the CD, and 90,000 dollars the next year of the CD. As the shortest CD matures, it can be used to buy longer-term CDs with higher interest rate. That process allows missing out on higher returns if the interest rates continually rise. Laddering also allows earning more revenue and flexibility. When each CD matures, you do not have the alternative to renew the rate or use its revenues for other things.

When to Buy a CD

A short-term CD may be a good alternative for funds that you plan to spend after the maturity date on something such as a house downpayment or even a vacation, even if it is a small amount. You need to check the interest rating on several high yield savings and money market accounts as they could pay a return that is similar to more than a short-term certificate of deposit without having you sacrifice quick access to your money. The biggest reason to buy a certificate of deposits would be when you have a large amount of revenue that you would like to keep safe while still earning just a bit more interest than one would if they had a savings or money market type of account. This could be the case if one is retired or is risk-averse to the investment of any funds into the financial market. The balance of reward and apparent risk is an ongoing struggle which the investors and savers continually face, especially when the interest rates are low. The Certificate of deposits does not give a big return on revenue though they are one of the sure things, as they basically have zero amount of risk attached.

Investing in a Certificate of Deposits while Rates are Low

Certificates of deposits provide for a higher interest provision as compared to the actual money markets. There are people who would complain about the sub 2 percent CD ratings when they are actually 5 to 10 times higher than the revenue from the money markets which operates between 0.2 and 0.3 percent interest rates. Earning 0.2 percent a year is quite a travesty if there is another option of earning up to 2 percent on revenue invested at lower risk. Diversification is also significant to the process. Placing 30 percent of the recurrent savings within the certificates of deposits is prudent and also gives you 70 percent in order to invest in the stock market, real estate or even yourself. It is really uplifting to buy a stock and it succeeds significantly, especially if it was represented as a rising technological tool in the market. But knowing how the economy ebbs and flows, this would be very much short-lived and should be treated with caution. The current economic environment is rather very risky and volatile. As such, the Federal Reserve has begun raising interest rates. Greece reached a point of defaulting on its debts resulting in an economic collapse which also happened in Venezuela. The Chinese stock market also recently took a small tumble and is perpetually getting halted for limiting down to 7 percent. During this time, Puerto Rico is also having debt issues while the United States stock market is consistently varying up and down with the NASDAQ. It would be much more prudent to use certificates of deposits as compared to risky but potentially profitable options presented by the stock or Forex market.

Strategies when using CDs

Using Short Maturities

When the rates are low, the fixed income investors have increased interest rate risk. If the interest rate goes up, then the investors only have underperforming investments to maturity or they try and sell them. However, this is done unfortunately at a loss. Though the owners of the Certificate of deposit could have the ability to sell theirs, the likely scenario would be that they would have to break the terms and conditions and then take the early withdrawal penalty. This would, in effect, eliminate the years of interest or it could even eat into the main investment depending on how bad the penalty is. For one to minimize the risk of the interest rates, you should look for CDs that have a shorter maturity as opposed to stretching for yield.

Evaluating Options like the Bumping up of the Certificate of Deposit

There are CDs which are better suited to the current low rate environment as compared to others. If the interest rates rise, then a bump up on the certificate of deposit allows the owner to seek a rate increase. With the interest rates potentially increasing again towards the end of 2018, longer term bumps for the CDs may be what is needed for investors that are concerned about looking for yield and interest rate risk. However, they could be hard to arrive at. Rates on the bump up CDs are usually competitive with the traditional CDs, but they are less than a special promotional rate.

Use of Short CD Laddering

Investors can mitigate the interest rate risks and capitalize on the higher yields for longer maturities and thus, increase the liquidity through splitting of the savings among the certificates of deposits for maturities that vary. This has already been covered in laddering when we discussed the use of two, three or even five-year maturities. As the one year CD matures, the proceeds, in this case, can be recycled back into the ladder with the purchase of another year or two-year CD. Considering the uncertainty of the timing of the next rate hike, it would be sensible to start with shorter ladders and extend it after the rates increase or just maintain the same period going forward.

Consider Indexed or Structured CDs

The structured CD is linked to other investments like the currency or stock market. Though they are not going to lose money because they are held to maturity, the returns are usually capped at a percentage of the total return of the underlying index or basket of securities. If it happens to be linked to the Standard & Poor index and this index returns 10 percent over the course of the year, then a structured certificate of deposit could provide three-quarter of this. It may vary among the products. This is a critic of the structured versions, as they can be quite complicated. However, there is a higher potential for greater returns as investors are pulled in. There are more downsides as the value of the investment can dip year by year. Apparently, you can lose money if you sell early. The drop in value is not necessarily because of volatility within the underlying investments but because of the limited demand for these certificates of deposits on the secondary market.

Being Aware Of Early Withdrawal Penalties

The early withdrawal penalties vary depending on the financial institutions. According to early withdrawal penalty surveys done by Bankrate, the penalty for breaking the CD early may reach as high as 4 percent of the amount that was withdrawn. Some are not that grievous. The usual penalty for early withdrawal for a long-term certificate of deposit is equal to six months' worth of interest. For the certificates of deposit that have a maturity of less than a year, the average penalty would equal to three months' worth of interest.

Take Care When Stretching For Yield

One of the objectives of the monetary policy of the Federal Reserve since the financial crisis has been to push investors into investments that are riskier. As such, the individuals that want or require higher yields could take on higher risk than they would be able to afford. Investors that require the preservation principal to live have to be careful about the investments they buy in order to meet the needs of the income. The dividend stocks, notes, and bonds have become de facto alternatives for certificates of deposits because of low-interest rates, though they are far from being an equivalent of CDs. The risk issued to the principal, in this case, can be very high.

Barbell Strategies

A barbell is another certificate of deposit strategy. It resembles the laddering method, though the middle rungs are not there. Short maturities are one end of the barbell. Furthermore, the investors could even place money in a high yield savings account to keep some of the principal more liquid. The long-term maturities are the other end of the barbell.

Shopping Around

Online banks and the credit unions could also offer a higher yield as compared to the traditional financial institutions. The local banks could provide a higher yield as compared to the national banks as well. Also, any type of institution could run these specials based on their own needs for revenue. This is why; it would be advisable to shop for the best CD rates.

Mistakes to Avoid With Certificates Of Deposit

Maximization of the certificate of deposit earnings would require more than opening the most convenient or obvious certificates. If you are not careful, there are as many pitfalls as there are opportunities. So you have to be careful in order to avoid the certificate of deposit mistakes.

Do Not Buy Long-Term CDs Which You Cannot Exit

Considering the fluctuations are going upwards currently and within the next few years, committing to the present rates for a long cycle of up to 5 years could be counter-productive in the end as the cycle will come back to a low soon. First, you may under-earn on the future yields by a significant margin during the later years as the rates climbed. The other thing is locking in your funds for a long period of time prevents one from moving into better-paying CDs which arrive. In the era of rising rates, flexibility and liquidity offer an individual an edge, and so you should always be ready to review early withdrawal penalties for any bank, especially when considering the opening of a certificate of deposit. The typical penalty can go up to six months interest and up to 5 years on a certificate of deposit. This is a significant figure in exchange for having the ability to move the revenue to a CD which pays better. Though the other institutions could even charge 12 months interest. There are some that even assess penalties which may subtract from the principal.

Placing Revenue into the Wrong CDs

Certificates of deposits are one of the smart places for money that you would not require during the short-term but are not convenient in placing in riskier places such as Forex or the stock exchange. The investors can make a mistake in either direction. Placing revenue into CDs which you may need in the short-term will land you an early withdrawal penalty that could remove the benefits that had been gained through the opening of the CD instead of the usual savings account. Though if you are holding money for five years, then many advisers will say that there is a need to invest in stocks. At the presently depressed returns, there are high chances that it is going to do better during the long-term. This advice may change if the returns climb to levels which are better since it would then be a worthy option.

Putting All the Funds in One Place

When the experts start talking about diversity, they would mean dividing the investment to different areas like the domestic and foreign stocks and CDs. Though, holding a diverse portfolio of the CDs with different maturity periods is also significant. The basic way to do this is by laddering or buying certificates in increasing terms. That gives a regular supply of the CDs which can then be reinvested at a higher return. It is also advisable to diversify across banks. If you are placing everything in one financial institution, there are a number of things which can go wrong including bankruptcy or insolvency or economic crisis. For example, the situation in Greece reached a point where people were only allowed to withdraw an amount of $63 per day to take care of their expenses to prevent a rush at the banks.

Letting you CD roll over automatically

When the CD approaches the stage of maturity, the bank will give you a notification that the term is coming to an end. If you do not do anything, then the financial institution will automatically roll the proceeds of the expired CD into a new certificate of deposit with a similar term. Letting the bank do this is usually always a mistake. You should choose the terms of the certificate of deposit wisely according to what is going on with the Federal Reserve. Because there is a 3 year CD maturing does not mean that you should opt to replace it with another for the same period of time.

Benefits and Disadvantages of CDs

CD Interests Can Get Higher Than the Savings Account Rates

The interest rates are commonly higher compared to the interest earned on the traditional savings account. The certificate of deposit will make you invest for a set period. Usually, the longer that the CD term will be, the higher the interest rate the bank is going to offer. The interest rate can be paid at the end of the CD or at the regular intervals during the term.

Fixed rate of interest

The CDs are the safest investments when it comes to the rates of interest because it usually stays fixed provided that there is an adequate laddering or the term of maturity is short for the CD. As such, you need not worry about the floating rate of interest.

Building Interest with a CD ladder

When you establish a CD ladder, you then invest in a group of CDs which mature at different periods. This provides one with regular access to some of the revenue without penalty while the rest proceeds to earn interest. You may then set up the CDs so that at least one of them can mature each year or you may decide to set them according to a quarterly basis. For example, you could decide to invest in one year and two year CD. When one year certificate of deposit matures, then it can be cashed out, and then you may decide to access the second CD during the next year.

Capitalizing On the Fixed Interest Rates When the Market Drops

The CD interest rates are locked in for the term of the certificate of deposit. That means that even if the market drops, you will still be getting the same interest for the complete term of the CD. If you happen to be concerned about the drop in the market or you are close to the point of retirement and want something that is conservative, then the CD would be the ideal alternative.

Low-Risk Investments with FDIC Insurance

They are considered as a low-risk investment especially when the investment is done at a bank or credit union. The CDs have insurance that could go up to $250,000. That would mean that if the banking institution fails, the money is then assured by the FDIC, and you will not lose the revenue that had been invested. You should note that the amount insured is inclusive of the account that one would have in your name at the bank.

Disadvantages

The disadvantages of the CD investment strategy include the potential loss of purchasing power and low liquidity because of inflation. One cannot redeem part or all of the CD account without the loss of accrued interest and potentially the principal. You need to check the CD account agreement in order to determine the penalties in the event that it would be pertinent to cash out at an earlier time. The money market mutual funds along with treasury bonds could be the better alternatives if you have to access revenue in an emergency. Strong economic growth usually leads to a point of inflation as well that can result in pressure for the short and the long-term interest ratings. However, the CD rates usually take a while before they catch up to the rising rates, so you might be earning less income as compared to some of the other fixed-income investments. There is zero capital gains potential on the regular CDs though some institutions provide the certificates of deposits which give a way to participate in the gains of the stock market.

Locked rates

The interest rates for the certificates of deposits may not keep up with the long periods of inflation. During the time, the interest earnings do not keep up with the rate of inflation that would, in turn, mean that the investment is losing the purchasing power during that period. When the rates are equal to the inflation, then the revenue will have the same amount of spending power. If the rates of interest are higher than the inflation, then you would be gaining interest from the investment. However, this usually happens the other way around.

Time deposit limits the ability to adjust investment strategy

When investing within the certificate of deposit, you are effectively investing for a particular period of time. The bank locks in the certificate of deposit for a particular duration and if the market improves, then you will, unfortunately, be linked in at the lower interest rates. The CDs thus limit the ability of the investor to move the funds to investments that are more lucrative as the market takes a turn for the better or worse. On the other hand, the banks could make the CD callable. This allows the banks the chance to cancel the CD in the event that the rates drop to a low level. You will still get the amount that you had earned, but you may have to reinvest in a certificate of deposit that has a lower interest rate.

Index-linked CDs

The index-linked CDs, which are also known as the market-linked or equity-linked CDs, give one regular interest payments and the chance to participate in the gains of the market index like the S&P 500 index. The FDIC still presently assures the principal, but there is a chance of losing a portion of that amount if you redeem one of the CDs before the time of maturity. The one that issues it could impose a limit on the amount that a person can earn. It could also have the right to buy back the CDs before the time of maturity and that would mean a lower return on investment.

The FDIC would recommend that you go through the disclosure statements before embarking on CD investment. You need to also consider that FDIC insurance is only applicable for the CDs that are given by the FDIC insured banking institutions. The other investment alternations that have similar risk-reward profiles include things such as the money markets and the treasury bonds that will be discussed in the following chapters.

Chapter 3: Money Markets

Source: http://getupwise.com/finance/investments/stocks-mutual-fund/10-ways-make-money-stock-market-without-investment/

What is a money market?

Money Markets can be confusing for the average person, especially if finances are not your cup of tea. But because money is so valuable, you will also need to learn about money markets. To start, the money market is a branch of financial markets where securities with a short-term maturity period are negotiated or bargained for by the interested parties. The participants of the money market participate through borrowing and lending these short-term and high-quality securities which often have maturities ranging from one year or less. To be candid, it is where financial instruments that are characterized by high liquidity and a short maturity period are traded. Because it is fully financed, it is easy to think that it is a physical market. However, it is not. Instead, it is a wireless, informal network linked through a digital aspect of fax machines, computers, and telephones. The link is between banks and traders both in the United States and other countries. To individuals, the money market gives them the opportunity to invest small to large amounts of money in a low-risk market. To larger institutions such as banks, NGOs, and the government, the money market is a means to sell the short-term securities that eventually helps to fund the short-term cash flow needs. The trading process is usually wholesale and over the counter meaning that it stays between or among financial companies and institutions and not individuals. However, individuals are still offered a chance to invest smaller amounts into these assets.

Money Market Instruments

The money market has a number of instruments that allow it to function properly. That is the buying and selling. They include treasury bills, securities lending and repurchase agreements (repos), interbank loans (loans between banks), bank accounts, and certificates of deposit. They are different in terms of how they are acquired, treated, and of course, traded under the financial regulatory law. They are also different in terms of how much the lender is reliant on the value of underlying collateral and not on the assessment of the party borrowing the security. The first and most common instrument is the bank deposits. They are not considered securities with the exception of certificates of deposits which are sometimes traded as securities under the right circumstances. As for interbank loans, they are a risky instrument because they are not secured by collateral and so when using them, the lender is completely reliant on the borrower's creditworthiness and not the assess repayment probability.

The second instrument is Treasury Bills which are popularly known as T-bills. Treasury bills are short-term notes that are issued by the US government that are later bought and sold by interested parties. They are considered one of the safest methods to hold short-term savings. Once they are issued by the US government, they undergo the process of being sold at a discount fee to what we can call 'the wholesale buyers'. They then reach the 'retail buyers' through a series of auctions and induction in the secondary market. The auctions function just as regular auctions would. The purchasers participate in a competitive bidding process which is, of course, risky because the bills may not be available at the bid price. The purchasers of the bills are usually broker-dealers, pension funds, individual investors, insurance companies, banks, and other large institutions. T-bills are made with three main lengths of maturity such as 90 days, 180 days, and 360 days. The 90- and 180-day bills are auctioned weekly, while the annual bills are auctioned monthly.

Another instrument is the Federal Agency notes. They are issued by some agencies but are not backed by the government. They are both short-term and long-term and offer higher yields than T-bills while retaining the risk default as very small. Agency notes are actively traded in the money market. However, they do not compare to T-bills in terms of marketing and as such, only corporations purchase these notes. The fourth instrument is the Commercial Paper which has a few similar themes to government office notes. Commercial paper is short-term promissory notes that are issued by both non-monetary and money related enterprises. They are short-term and are issued by extensive companies that are credit-commendable and have unused lines of bank credit implying that they convey low default chance. A business paper is novel, since it doesn't expect banks to go about as intermediaries between purchasers and dealers. Rather, it is issued straightforwardly by well-established companies and huge money-related foundations. The part of banks for this situation is to go about as operators for the exchange. They don't expect any foremost position and are not committed in the reimbursement of the business paper. With regards to an offering, organizations offer business paper. However, merchants charge an expense and handle the whole procedure of exchanging funds from the loan specialist to the borrower. Commercial paper is lawfully viewed as a debt without collateral. Consequently, in the United States, it has maturity dates ranging from 1 to 270 days. They are issued in groups from $10,000 to $1 million which are considered too huge for retail financial specialists.

Fifth is the Bankers' Acceptances. They are short-term and are delivered by a non-money related company for the sake of a bank. Acceptances are made by a drawer to give the conveyor a privilege to the cash as demonstrated on the predefined date. Usually, they are utilized in a universal exchange. That way, it can profit from both the carrier and the drawer. In any case, it isn't restricted to universal exchange as they can be utilized when organizations buy products using a credit card or when they have to fund stock. Holders of acceptances can offer it on a secondary market where financial specialists can benefit from the short-term speculation.

Acceptances have a development length of somewhere in the range of one and a half year from the date of issue.

The sixth instrument is the Testaments of Stores. They are ordinarily issued by a government-sanctioned bank. They are issued against kept funds which gain a predetermined return for an unequivocal timeframe. This way, they are considered as a kind of enthusiasm bearing 'time stores'. The procedure is straightforward. An individual or organization loans the bank a picked measure of cash for a settled timeframe. In return, the bank consents to reimburse the cash with the premium it would include procured inside that time. Evidently put, the declaration comprises the bank's consent to reimburse the credit. The rate of development on these declarations goes from thirty days to a half year or more, while the measure of the face esteem can change significantly. An early withdrawal of funds, more often than not, comprises to a punishment except for if the first buyer needs access to the cash before the development date in which case, the CDs can be sold to another speculator. There are gigantic testaments of stores that range from $100,000 or more which are more debatable and pay higher financing costs than smaller categories. They are just safeguarded by the FDIC for up to $100,000. Compact discs can likewise come as Eurodollar. They are debatable declarations that are issued against US dollar commitments as a rule in a remote branch of a residential branch. Since specialists bargain in huge aggregates, the CDs that are facilitated, as a rule, pay higher financing costs while offering more liquidity than the CDs that are obtained specifically from a bank.

At long last, we have the Repurchase Agreements normally known as Repos. It is a type of security where you pitch consent to repurchase it at a higher cost and in a later date. It is a short-term increase that acts as treasury securities that are exchanged through buying from a merchant, at which point consents to an arrangement expressing that the securities will be bought at a higher cost from a merchant. These agreements are exceedingly fluid, extending for twenty hours to a couple of months. In numerous viewpoints, repo understandings are fundamentally the same as bank store accounts and in that capacity, numerous companies guarantee that their banks exchange the overabundance of cash for such funds, naturally.

Money Market Accounts

This is a record that is enthusiasm-bearing, that has attributes of both a checking and a bank account. The distinction is that money market accounts normally pay a financing cost that is higher than the bank account, and furthermore, furnishes the holder of the record with restricted registration capacity. They require considerably higher least stores and parities. However, in the meantime, they offer a more alluring loan fee. While considering a currency showcase account, contrasting rates is a basic initial step despite the fact that MMA loan fees have verifiably been higher than those of the fundamental investment accounts. At present, they are generally the same. Money market accounts are guaranteed by the Federal Deposit Insurance Corp. or the FDIC at banks and the National Credit Union Administration or NCUA at credit associations.

They were first made by banks to offer more focused financing costs than those on investment accounts. They turned out to be broadly well-known in the mid-1980s. It was when loan fees ascended into the twofold digits. This gave investors a chance to create high, hazard-free returns. The contributing stores for Money Market Accounts are frequently held in instruments, for example, government securities, testaments of a store, and business paper which offer higher yields than those found in bank accounts.

A money market account is a decent method to contribute your cash on the off chance that you are searching for generally safe speculation designs. Like checking and bank accounts, MMAs are store accounts which are safeguarded by the Federal Deposit Insurance Corporation. The FDIC protects the accounts by restricting the withdrawals to six withdrawals for each month. On the off chance that in excess of six withdrawals were to occur in multi-month, the bank would charge an expense or control the record status into a non-enthusiasm bearing financial records. The tradeoff for higher rates is regularly a higher store necessity, thus with numerous MMAs, the record needs to keep up a day-by-day base to get the most astounding accessible loan cost.

While picking an MMA, it is great to direct your examination and go for the best one. An MMA requires a considerable amount of cash to open. It could cost as low as $1,000 to as much as $10,000, with the end goal of opening a record and sidestepping the charges. With respect to loan fee, an MMA procures enthusiasm in a way that resembles a bank account. As indicated by the FDIC, the national normal yearly rate yield or APY for a Money Market Account is 0.10% as of March 2018. With an MMA, you will get a platinum card and checks, making your record less demanding to get to, which isn't the situation with an ordinary investment account or a CD.

One of the advantages of having an MMA is that it is not like money market finance. It won't lose esteem if the market falls since it is sponsored up to $250,000 per investor by the FDIC or NCUA. To guarantee your funds are secure, you should dependably utilize a money market account from your confided bank or a credit association. You should also ask your bank or credit association to check that your funds are guaranteed, and keep your stores underneath the most extreme secured limits. MMAs are valuable for cash in case you need it immediately. They enable you to win a little return while keeping the funds protected and available for substantial, rare costs, for example, crisis funds, paying doctor's facility bills, educational cost, and understudy advances while planning for quarterly expense installments. It isn't the best place to put funds that you will often require sooner rather than. These are more suited for funds such as home loans so that they could gain more interest.

Advantages of Money Market Accounts

1. With the FDIC insurance, you can be sure that your money will be here when you need it and even when the market falls. It is truly a low-risk investment plan that allows you to get emergency funds when you really need them

2. Even though the account does have a limit on the number of times you can withdraw per month, it is still easy to withdraw money immediately, any time, for any reason, by transferring into them into your checking or regular savings account.

3. An obvious advantage of MMAs is the higher interest rates that they have compared to the regular savings accounts. You will notice better rewards with this type of account.

4. Another favorite advantage is that even when the interest rate falls, you can move the funds into your account without any fees for the purpose of withdrawing the funds and placing them into other investments.

5. You may also connect the money market deposit to the account and then buy treasuries and bonds via phone to the account.

Disadvantages of Money Market Accounts

1. The most obvious and probably most hindering disadvantage of a money market account is that it has a limited number of withdrawals per month. This can be really inconvenient for you, especially if the matter is urgent.

2. In order for you to avoid paying monthly account fees, monitor the minimum amount every month, which can be a little expensive and hard to achieve if something were to suddenly happen to your finances.

3. Like the limited number of withdrawals you can make per month, you may also only receive a limited number of checks every monthly period. Most accounts only allow three checks per month with a fine for exceeding this number. This, of course, leads up to inconvenience.

4. If you fail to maintain your minimum fee per month, you will not only be charged a particular fee, the interest will also be going reduced. This, of course, will force you to move your funds to a different account, because you will not be earning as much as you used to.

5. Unfortunately, being insured by FDIC is not all good. With its security comes a paradox consequence where the interest rates on money market deposit accounts are lower than what you can earn through money market funds.

6. The interest rates for money market accounts can be tiered which means that they are dependent on the account.

    You may only qualify for the highest level if you have $10,000 or a higher level interest rate of the deposit which of course could not be easily afforded by anyone. What is worse is that the interest of the account also goes up and down without guarantee for any time period. Therefore, to some extent, it is unreliable.

7. Like almost every other form of money you receive, the interest received within the market or other account reduces because of the federal taxation. At the same time, inflation makes the buying power go down if the interest rate is less than the inflation.

8. Finally, even though the money market is a great low-investment plan, it is not suitable for people with long-term objectives. This is because it doesn't have a set term and provides revenue.

Money Market Funds

Money market funds refer to those which are fixed in income and investment as well as in debt securities attributed to short maturities and reduced credit risk. They have a very low potential for volatility. It entails securities which are short-term or less than a year such as liquid debt and monetary instruments. There are times that investors can buy shares of the funds from the money market through mutual funds and banks. The purpose of MMFs is to give investors a better place so they can invest as opposed to cash-equivalent assets and unlike MMAs. MMFs are attributed as lower risk and low-return type of investment. Because of the low returns, money market funds are seldom used as an investment for the long-term, because it does not allow them to reach their financial goals.

MMFs are often considered by investors who either have an investment goal with a short time horizon or for those who have lower tolerances. These are also for investors who are trying to diversify with a conservative investment. They are also considered by investors who need the investment to be extremely liquid.

Advantages of Money Market Funds

1. Stability - This is apparently a lower volatility type of mutual fund. MMFs are very stable.
2. Security - Because they are short-term investments, they are not as prone to the fluctuations of the market as opposed to other investments.
3. Liquidity - Assets are liquid which makes it a lot easier to clear brokerage account trades for other savings made, or to get funds from the money market fund. They become available by the next day.

Disadvantages of Money Market Funds

1. Inflation - The short-term nature of underlying investments can be affected by inflation resulting in lower returns as compared to the investment.
2. Credit risk - Unlike MMAs, MMFs are not insured via the FDIC. This means that you are constantly at risk of losing money and of course, your interest rate.

In conclusion, despite its cons, the money market is a good low-risk investment plan that can earn you some extra funds in interest. However, before you engage in it or any other form of investment, it is always good to conduct a thorough research, especially if you are a newbie to the financial game. To help you get started, you can follow the following tips to keep you from losing money and capitalize on your investment to the fullest.

1. To begin, make sure that you keep your money market account at the same bank as your checking accounts. This will make it easier to transfer funds between them which will eventually give you the ultimate convenience.
2. Like any other money you receive, you should make a budget for your MMA. It is the best way to free up more money to put into savings accounts or to create a budget. You should also make sure that it is a realistic budget that you can stick with. If you cannot do it by yourself, consult with an institution that offers money market accounts.
3. Another tip is to create and maintain saving goals for yourself. The Consumer Financial Protection Bureau recommends paying yourself first before you pay off your other bills. It is highly recommended that you always prioritize your savings. Take advantage of the online savings calculators that the banks offer to help you establish reasonable saving plans.
4. Before you even open an MMA, ensure that you have read and made yourself familiar with all the fees such as penalties, new account fees, and the like. Always look for one with low annual expenses that will not drag down your rate of return.
5. Because we are moving into the digital world, make use of the technology as well as apps. There are several apps out there that will not only help you with the money market but can also enhance your savings and interest rates. For example, Stash is an investment app that automatically deducts money from your account and invests it in one of 30 investment options on your behalf. What's more is that you only need $5 minimum to get started.

Chapter 4: Compound Interest

Compound Interest refers to the process where one generates more return on the asset when it is reinvested. In order to be effective, there are two things that are needed. These include the reinvestment of time and earnings. Compound interest may assist the initial to grow in an exponential manner, and it is one of the greatest investing tools available. This is not a new term in the investment world as the concept has been around for some time. Compounding has been referred to as the 8th wonder of the world by Einstein and has also gotten acclaimed from other prominent figures such as Warren Buffet and Benjamin Graham as one of the major investment principles.

According to Buffet in one of the letters written to his investment partners, it is the most powerful tool in the creation of wealth through investment. Compounding happens when the returns of an investment are placed back in the cycle in order to come up with returns. The results, over the course of time, have initiated a snowball effect where the portfolio begins growing quite rapidly the longer that it is reinvested. The catch though is that compounding needs patience and time. However, these are the things that scare a number of modern-day investors that operate in the high-speed reality.

This is earning interest on the interest that was already earned yesterday. It is like blowing inside a balloon and as you keep inflating it, it only gets bigger. On the other hand, if you had been blowing air into the balloon while also letting the air out from a different hole, the balloon does not get to become as big as it could potentially be. The returns that are created from continuously reinvesting the returns is what is referred to as the compound gains. That is what people who have created wealth for themselves have utilized and one of the main logical reasons as to why the claim the rich get richer is very true. These returns that you are reinvesting may be from the interest gotten from a bank, crowd-funding or profit from the sale of shares and dividends from a business. So long as the discipline of reinvesting most of the profits or the returns is there, then compound interest is going to work out in your best interest.

Now when it comes to money management, the more risk that one is willing to accept, the higher the returns they can usually get. Over the course of time, placing revenue into stocks provides a higher return on the investment as opposed to putting it into a savings account. After the onset of the financial crisis during 2008, there were a number of people who became allergic to risk, so to speak, so they opted to settle for a lower level of returns in order to decrease the level of risk. The issue was that placing the revenue into ordinary savings accounts would keep it safe but the returns from such an investment would possibly not even be enough to keep up with the level of inflation. While one ought to have ordinary savings account for the sake of emergencies, placing the money in investments of a higher risk nature has the potential of assisting in long-term financial prospects.

The formula for the calculation of returns according to a flat interest rate that is compounded once per year is

$$\text{Total return} = \text{initial investment} * (1+i)^n$$

This is where i= is the interest rate and n would be the number of years that the money is invested.

While the formula oversimplifies compounding because the interest rates fluctuate and the saving vehicles compound more than just once every year, it can illustrate how strong the compounding process is. The interest rate is the main determinant as to how much the initial investment grows.

Things That Determine the Compound Interest Returns

There are three elements which impact the rate of revenue compounds, and these include time, the interest rate, and the taxation rate.

1. The interest rate is earned on the investment or the gains. If one is investing in the stocks, then this becomes the total profit from the dividends and the capital gains.
2. There is also the time because the longer that money could remain uninterrupted, the bigger the principal may grow. This is not any different from growing plants. Usually, the plant may continue to grow every day and will be bigger when it is a year old as compared to when it was five months old.
3. The tax rate and the timing are about the taxation that is to be issued to the government. You may end up with a lot more money if you do not have to pay the taxes in the first place or up to the end of the year. That is why accounts like the Traditional IRA or the SEP IRA are very significant.

Compound interest and the time value for revenue

The concept of compound interest is the foundation concerning the time value of money which implies that the value of the money changes to an individual dependent on when it is attained. For example, earning $1,000 at the present will be preferable to earning the same amount of money in the future. If you have it in hand, then it is possible to invest it, so as to generate some sort of dividends or interest income. Then afterward, it is possible to spend it on the things that you would like such as payment of debt to lower the interest expenditure that you have. When you consider the time value of money, you will find formulas showing the calculation of compound interest.

Compound Interest over the course of time

The optimum way that one can get to understand the concepts would be placing them in a compound interest table which illustrates how substantially the wealth can be hindered or grown through small alterations over the course of time. Take, for example, there is an investor that sets aside 5,000 dollars. If the money is invested at a rate of 5% per annum and is held over a period of five years, it will return $6,381.4 over the course of those five years. Once this becomes clear, then it becomes evident that saving money solely does not explain why individuals have a bigger fortune as compared to other people.

As attractive as all this seems, you should not fall prey to the temptation which can arise from getting higher returns by risking more. One glance at the compound interest chart for the principal that you would like to put in, and you would want to do whatever it takes in order to earn a higher rate of return which can go as high as 20 percent potentially. That could be quite dangerous in the long run. Unless you know what you are doing regardless of how successful the endeavor is during the initial stages, you should avoid the potential of wiping yourself out. In finance, 20 to 60 percent returns during the initial years are quite good, but if there happens to be a potential for negative 80 to 100 percent somewhere there, then that will be an end to itself because all the capital will be gone and without capital, there is no way of making investments.

Benefits and disadvantages of compound interest

Managing the fluctuations in cash flows is challenging for many individuals and business owners. Saving and investing even a small part of the revenue that is in a compound interest structure could assist with maintaining profitability over the long-term. On the other hand, there is the consideration that over leveraging oneself within such an account could expose one to financial difficulty going forward.

The Concept

As a concept, compounding means earning interest on the money that you save and also on the interest that was earned. If the business invests 10,000 dollars into an account, then it is going to earn on both the principal and the profit that has been gained from the interest percentage as a total.

Practical considerations

The longer that the revenue sits within the compound interest account, the more it is going to benefit the business during the long-term. The number of times that the interest is compounded is a significant difference in the degree of advantage that the compound interest avails. Investments where the interests compounds on a yearly basis will probably grow slower as compared to the investment where the interest compounds according to a quarterly or even monthly basis.

Saving benefits

Understanding the concept for compounding the interest can be just as significant for saving revenue as it is what the business is able to make from investing the money. If the business usually uses credit cards and does not pay the balance in full every month, then the interest is then calculated with the use of compound interest.

Dividend Investing

The investor could take advantage of reinvesting in a number of means. The dividend reinvestment can be utilized by firms and corporations. It doesn't give the DRIP for the stock. The dividends can be taken and then reinvested with additional funds that may increase the overall returns over the long run. Furthermore, there are some ways of gaining an advantage from a compound interest in terms of dividends.

Disadvantages: When It Becomes an Issue

With regards to loans, the interest built on the original amount can be hard to consider. The reason for the increase in payment of the loan is because of the compounding interest. As such, compound interest can be a double-edged sword as it can be used to garner revenue from both the debt and the interest that is used to pay that debt. The cost of compound interest is disguised and can get away with the money that you have. Missing on payments by even a day could mean that the interest falls so that it is calculated even before the payment is recorded. Compound interest is usually designed in order to assist the lenders. The credit card monthly repayments usually set up in such a way so that you are encouraged to keep borrowing and so you can keep paying interest. You might eat the capital owed by repaying the interest plus some capital each time. Thus compound interest is regarded as some of the worst kind of usury and was actually condemned by roan law and the common laws of several countries.

Overall, compound interest is effective when in favor of investments, though it can also be cumbersome when it is a loan. The best thing to do is to stay on top of the payments and not let interest accrue on debts because they feed off each other in an exponential manner when it comes to compound interest.

Chapter 5: Treasury Bonds

The treasury bonds are utilized for the purpose of investing, especially when it comes to retirement. However, experts claim that every investor can benefit from the bond exposure. Bonds having reliability and a lot of steady returns are able to stabilize and even improve the portfolio. When the volatility of the stock market gets to the place where it makes individuals not comfortable, it is the stability given by treasury bonds that most often quells the inclination of making hasty decisions.

Taking this into perspective, bonds are loans that the holder gives to an issuer as an exchange for the principal of the investor added to the interest. Governments, corporations, and municipalities all give bonds for the purpose of financing the projects and activities. When bonds are bought, you then become creditors for the issuer. When bonds are purchased, then you become a creditor. This is a distinction between the bonds and stocks. As such, you have the potential ability to own a part of the corporation. As a part owner, regardless of the scale of the investment, you get to be a participant in the profits, dividends and get an appreciation concerning the apparent share price.

Treasury bonds happen to be issued in dollar denominations which are usually at 1,000 dollars for the corporate bonds. That is the face value that you need to pay for it. The date that the bond is first sold is known as the issue date, and the date the principal is due is called the maturity date. So, the bonds are issued and will eventually reach the stage of maturity. During these two dates, the issuer can make regular interest payments which are known as coupons. The bond interest is known as a coupon because before the trading was done electronically, the investors had to deal with paper certificates when they bought a bond and attached to each of the certificates were coupons for these payments.

How the Bond Pays Interest

The issuers utilize the maturity of the bond and the prevailing interest rates of the market to determine the competitive interest rate or the coupon rate. This is illustrated as an annual percentage of a face value. For example, a $2,000 bond that has a 10 percent semi-annual coupon will provide $200 of interest for each year in installments of 100 dollars each until it reaches its maturity. The bonds can have a floating or fixed interest rate. The fixed rates, as mentioned, stay the same. A floating interest rate, on the other hand, can be reset from time to time. It is considered as a percentage that is spread over the benchmark.

How the Interest Rates Affect the Prices of the Bond

At the time the bond is given, it can trade between investors within the secondary market. The bonds that are previously issued usually trade at discounts at the face value. This is what happens when the market interest rates alter as relative to the coupon rate of the bond. When the interest rates increase, the coupon rates on the new bonds also go upwards. This results in lower rates for the old bonds and becoming less appealing. In this case, the price investors are willing to pay for the drops of the older bonds. When the interest rate goes down, so does the price of the bonds which are older and which allow a higher coupon to rise. Bonds that trade at rates that are below the face value or equal to the set value are known as discount bonds. The bonds that trade above the face value are also referred to as the premium bonds. The price of the bond is usually quoted as the percentage that depends on the face value of the bond as expressed according to points. A discount bond is quoted at 90 points or trades at 90 percent of par which is also 900 dollars for a $1,000 bond. The premium bond would be at 110 points or trades at 110 percent of par, and this would be related as $1,100 for a $1,000 bond.

Why Invest In Them

Source: http://dragonflycap.com/a-deep-dive-into-us-treasuries/

There are three main reasons why people would consider buying treasury bonds. There are some investors that use them to initiate a steady income stream. Considering the coupon payments for the Treasury bond are something which is guaranteed, the investors then have the knowledge of when and how much it is going to receive. This institutes an element of predictability and reliability which can be used to base other business models. It also makes the bonds useful for the funding of particular future liabilities including the college or retirement funds. The principal repayment, after all, can be timed so as to coincide with the expenses or the purchases.

On the other hand, you might use the treasury bonds to stabilize the portfolio and its overall amount of risk. Bonds have low relation when compared to stocks and that means, the value is up when the stocks are down and vise versa. Because of this factor, high-quality bonds like high-grade corporate issues such as the government bonds can be utilized for the diversification of the risks of owning stocks. The bonds may also protect the portfolio from an economic decline. During an economic slowdown, the reducing inflation increases the purchasing power for bond payments in the future. In the same way, because the declining economy reduces the returns attained from the stocks, the investors then go to bonds, and this drives up the prices of their worth.

Bond Investment and Other Strategies

When looking to a bond investment strategy, it is crucial that you diversify your risk. You will want to do this through the creation of portfolios of different bonds with each different characteristic. If one issuer couldn't meet his obligations, the other issuers would pay the principal and interest. Choosing a bond from several options will help stave off losses within any of the market sectors.

Preserving the Principal and Earning Interest

When keeping the finances in check, the main objective would be earning interest. After that, you need to consider an approach to 'buy and hold'. When considering a bond and then holding it to the point of maturity, you can get interest dues at least twice a year and then get the face value when it matures. If what has been chosen is a premium bond and the coupon is higher than the interest rating, then you need to know that the amount attained at maturity is going to be lower than that which you had paid for the bond.

When you use the strategy of buy and hold, there is no need for concern over the effect of the interest rates on the market value or the pricing of the bond.

In the events that the rates and the value decrease, then you will not feel any impact unless the strategy alters and one tries to sell the bond. Just holding on to it would mean that you would not invest the principal at a higher rate.

If the bond chosen can be called, then you have taken risks of making the principal to return before it starts to mature. The bonds can be redeemed or called earlier by the issuer when the rates are going down. That would mean the investor could be forced to invest their amount at the lower rates. When you use the buy and hold approach, the thing to do includes:

- The yield to maturity or the yield to call as a higher amount of yields could mean a higher level of risk.
- The credit quality of the one that is issuing the bond: Bonds that have lower credit ratings may provide a higher yield. However, it also carries the risk that the issuer is not going to be able to keep their end of the bargain.

Management of the Interest Rate Risk

In the buy and hold, investors are able to manage the risk through the creation of the portfolio of bonds which are laddered with a number of different maturities that go from one to ten years. Portfolios which are laddered have the original amount to be returned at determined intervals. When the bond starts to mature, one would have the opportunities to reinvest proceeds during the long-term in the event that you want to keep it going. In the event that the rates will continue to increase, the principal, which is maturing, can be reinvested for profit. Though, if they decline, the portfolio would earn higher interest levels for the longer-term holdings. Using the barbell approach, one only invests within the short-term and the longer-term bonds as opposed to just the intermediates. These longer-term holdings should allow for coupon rates which are appealing. Having a bit of the principal maturing during the short-term allows for the chance to invest the revenue in another place if the bond market goes downwards.

Maximization of income

If the overall objective is to increase the interest income effectively, you may get higher coupons for bonds which are longer term. Because they have more time to reach the point of maturity, these longer-term bonds happen to be vulnerable to alterations in the interest rates. If you are oriented towards the 'buy and hold' strategy, these alterations are not going to affect you unless you alter the strategy and decide to just sell the bonds. You may also find higher coupon ratings for the corporate bonds as opposed to the treasury bonds with maturities that are comparable. The corporate scene allows bonds with lower credit ratings to pay higher income as compared to higher credits with similar maturities. The bonds which are high yield may provide coupon rates as the issuer had credits which are beneath investment grade. The lower the credit rating of the issuer, the larger the risk of defaulting on their obligations or not be able to pay the interest. If you want to invest in high yield bonds, you are also going to have to diversify the investments among several issuers so as to reduce the chance of the potential effect of defaulting from any one issuer. High yield bond prices are also vulnerable as compared to the other bond prices when it comes to economic downturns because of the periodic ebbs and flows which affect the interest settings and so the potential payout to the issuers.

Total Return

The use of bonds in order to invest in total return or combining capital appreciation and income needs a trading model that is aggressive and a perspective of the direction of how things are going, not to mention, the beforehand knowledge of the rates. Total return mode investors could purchase the bonds when pricing is down and then attempt selling when it increases. The prices go down when interest rates increase and as the economy proceeds to grow. They usually increase when the interest rates go down, usually as the Federal Reserve would try to jump-start things right after the recessions. In different areas of the market, a difference in the supply and demand can allow for short-term trading chances. Different options, futures, and derivatives may also be used for the sale of effective different market perspectives. There are bonds which have the total return as the main goal and this allows the chance for investors to benefit from market movements while leaving the investment decisions to professional managers.

Tax-Advantaged Investment

If you belong high on the tax bracket, then your goal could be the reduction of the interest income that can be taxed in order to get more money. The interest on several securities is usually taxed federally, though one is exempt at the local level. This becomes attractive for those living in the states that have high taxation. The municipal securities get a lot of interest, and this is exempted from the federal income tax and in some scenarios, it would be exempted from the state and local forms of taxation. Similarly, barbells, bullets, and ladders can be implemented for an approach which is tax advantaged. Buying of municipals within an account that is tax-deferred is counterproductive. Bond swapping would be the opposite of getting the taxation related objective especially for those investors holding a bond which has reduced in value, though it has capital gains which are taxable. In this case, the investor may opt to sell the original bond at a loss, and this can be used as a tradeoff for the taxable gain. They can buy another bond with the pricing for maturity and the coupons resembling the ones sold and that reestablishes the position.

Pros of Treasury Bonds

The main advantage, regardless of the name, is that all treasury securities have the backing of the government. This reduces the default risk considering the government may always be able to mint the revenue that can be used in the repayment of the treasury debt. They also have good liquidity. The market for treasuries is quite substantial and active which allows it to become easier to buy and sell the bonds in whichever quantity or maturity that you prefer. Similarly, the treasury is consistent in selling new treasury securities at auctions where the public regularly participates to buy them directly from the government. The treasury bonds also feature a guaranteed rate of return. Considering the backer is the government in terms of insurance, this is one of the most secure bets one can hedge. There are also tax exemptions as you will not have to pay state or even local tax on the interest that is attained after every six months. Finally, there is zero loss in value. The treasury bonds are seen as one of the safest or lowest risk type of investments. The government backs the initial investment, so short of a total economic collapse; you would not have anything to be worried about.

Cons of treasury bonds

They might be the safest examples, but there are also some issues that one has to contend with. For one, there is a longer-term investment for this bonds which could take as long as 30 years for them to mature. Sure the payoff is great, but it is too long a time to wait for in some circumstances. Fixed interest bonds also deny the chance for one to change their stance on the bond because you would have to be operating at the interest rate that was there initially when the bond was being issued. That will make you lose money if the interest rate goes up during the tenure before the maturity. There is also a tax liability. Even though you do not generally pay the state or the local taxes concerning the interest that the bonds generate, the interest could be subject to federal income taxation.

The other issue when it comes to treasury bonds is they are not sold as much from the American treasury. The treasury only sells about four instances every year. That would mean that if you would like to buy them on an auxiliary market, then you would have to avail yourself to buy them each time. The other potential issue is that the interest can only be credited to your account every six months. That does not allow you to access the funds at any time which is unfortunate and restricting for the most part.

www.ingramcontent.com/pod-product-compliance
Lightning Source LLC
Chambersburg PA
CBHW040336220526
45473CB00009B/2705